MEGA *MACHINES*

PAUL HARRISON

ARCTURUS

This edition published in 2012 by Arcturus Publishing Limited
26/27 Bickels Yard, 151–153 Bermondsey Street,
London SE1 3HA

Written by Paul Harrison
Edited by Joe Harris
Designed by sprout.uk.com and Matt Pull

ISBN: 978-1-84858-652-9
CH002414EN
Supplier 05, Date 0712, Print Run 1855

Printed in Singapore

CONTENTS

INTRODUCTION

Welcome to the finest collection of vehicles ever to be assembled! From super speedy bikes to the classiest cars, futuristic planes to colossal trucks, everything in this book is a marvel of engineering. Cool photographs of each one are on every page, with close ups to show special features and tons of stats and facts. So what are you waiting for? On your marks, get set, go!

SUPER

What makes a superbike 'super'? The motorcycles in this chapter have been taken to the extreme. They are faster, more expensive, more striking and more exclusive than any ordinary bike.

BIKES

200
210
220
230
240
270
280

MV-AUGUSTA F4CC

One of the rarest and most expensive bikes around today is the MV-Augusta F4CC. In fact this bike is so exclusive, there were only a hundred of them ever made!

The F4CC is based on Augusta's F4R. However, over 90% of the parts for the F4CC were made specially for it.

The F4CC uses brakes that are usually found on racing motorbikes.

The Italian firm MV-Augusta have been making racing motorbikes since 1954. The sporty F4CC continues on that path. The 'CC' in its name is the initials of the managing director of the firm, Claudio Castiglioni. He wanted to make a bike that he was proud to put his name to – the F4CC is the result of that dream.

The speed is limited to 315 km/h (195 mph) to protect the tyres from ripping apart.

The F4CC is made of light but strong materials, including titanium and carbon fibre.

SUPER STATS

MV-AUGUSTA F4CC
TOP SPEED: 315 km/h (195 mph)
WEIGHT: 187 kg (412.3 lbs)
ENGINE: 200 bhp
MADE IN: Italy
PRICE: £78,000

There are six gears – but you can travel at over 129 km/h (80 mph) in first!

ICON SHEENE

Superbikes often look like vehicles from the future. However, one of the rarest and most expensive superbikes has an old-fashioned styling – and the makers have done this on purpose. It is called the Icon Sheene, and it's the perfect mix of old and new.

Each Icon Sheene is built by hand. The fuel tank alone takes over a month to make.

Owners can buy an exclusive helmet to go with the bike. It will be painted by the same man who painted Barry Sheene's helmets.

The engine comes from the Japanese company Suzuki.

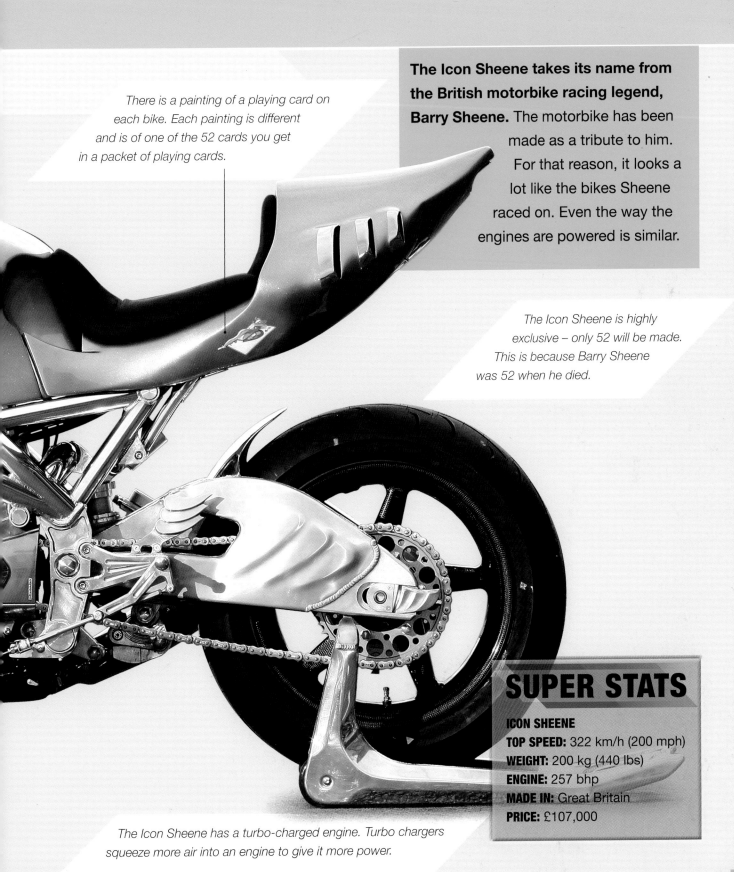

There is a painting of a playing card on each bike. Each painting is different and is of one of the 52 cards you get in a packet of playing cards.

The Icon Sheene takes its name from the British motorbike racing legend, Barry Sheene. The motorbike has been made as a tribute to him. For that reason, it looks a lot like the bikes Sheene raced on. Even the way the engines are powered is similar.

The Icon Sheene is highly exclusive – only 52 will be made. This is because Barry Sheene was 52 when he died.

SUPER STATS

ICON SHEENE
TOP SPEED: 322 km/h (200 mph)
WEIGHT: 200 kg (440 lbs)
ENGINE: 257 bhp
MADE IN: Great Britain
PRICE: £107,000

The Icon Sheene has a turbo-charged engine. Turbo chargers squeeze more air into an engine to give it more power.

DODGE TOMAHAWK

A superbike should be eye-catching – and no bike causes more double-takes than the Dodge Tomahawk. It may be one of the strangest looking superbikes around, but it is also one of the fastest.

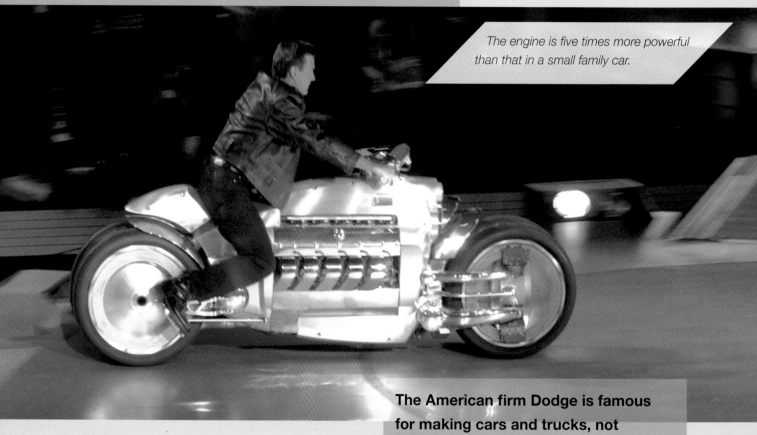

The engine is five times more powerful than that in a small family car.

The Tomahawk is made from aluminium, which is very light and very strong.

The American firm Dodge is famous for making cars and trucks, not bikes. That might explain the Dodge Tomahawk's odd looks. It's got four wheels like a car, not two wheels like a normal motorbike. Even the engine comes from a car – a super sports car also made by Dodge, called the Viper.

The Tomahawk may look great, but it is not legal to drive it on the road.

The wheels are grouped in two batches of two.

The engine sends the power to the two rear wheels.

The Tomahawk is a concept bike. That means it was never meant to be made in any great number. Instead it shows what could be possible in the future.

SUPER STATS

DODGE TOMAHAWK
TOP SPEED: estimated 483+ km/h (300+ mph)
WEIGHT: 680 kg (1500 lbs)
ENGINE: 500 bhp
MADE IN: USA
PRICE: £353,000

TOP 1 ACK ATTACK STREAMLINER

Some motorbikes are built purely for speed. The Ack Attack is designed to break records, while drag bikes go head-to-head in the fastest bike races on Earth.

Ack Attack has reached a top speed of an incredible 634 km/h (394 mph).

Ack Attack is built around two Suzuki Hayabusa engines (see pages 24-25).

The fastest motorbike in the world is called Top 1 Ack Attack. It is a type of bike called a streamliner. Streamliners have a completely enclosed body. This allows the air to pass around the bike more smoothly.

Ack Attack needs a parachute to help it slow down.

DRAG BIKES

Drag bikes can accelerate to 161 km/h (100 mph) in 1.1 seconds.

The fastest sports motorbikes on the planet are drag bikes. They compete in races along straight, quarter-mile (400 m) tracks. Some of them run on a special fuel called nitromethane.

A big wheel at the back of the bike provides lots of grip.

Some drag bikes have a long metal frame at the back called a wheelie bar. This stops the bike from tipping backwards.

SUPER STATS

TOP 1 ACK ATTACK STREAMLINER
TOP SPEED: 634 km/h (394 mph)
WEIGHT: 907 kg (2000 lbs)
ENGINE: 1100 bhp
MADE IN: USA
PRICE: Not for sale

KTM 690 RALLY

Most superbikes are designed for tearing around on a road or race track. However, some are built for much tougher terrain. Going off-road is a real test of how durable a bike can be. These superbikes show just how it should be done.

The strong chassis stays rigid. This makes the KTM 690 easier to drive at high speed on rough surfaces.

The KTM 690 Rally has six gears.

The KTM 690 is a purebred rally bike. It was designed to compete in some of the longest, toughest races in the world. The most famous is the Dakar Rally, a gruelling all-terrain race which can be over 8,000 km (5,000 miles) long. No problem for the KTM, though – it won the event three years in a row.

Suspension helps to smooth at bumps. The KTM hits some big bumps, so the suspension can move up and down by 300 mm (12 inches).

SUZUKI RM-Z450

Motocross racing sees bikes competing against each other on off-road courses. Sometimes these can be purpose-built indoor tracks, but the more powerful bikes race outdoors. One of the best motocross superbikes is the Japanese-made Suzuki RM-Z450.

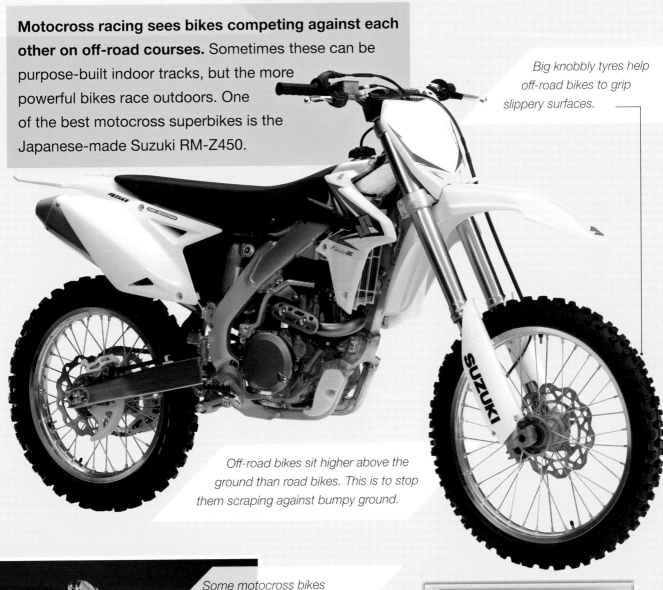

Big knobbly tyres help off-road bikes to grip slippery surfaces.

Off-road bikes sit higher above the ground than road bikes. This is to stop them scraping against bumpy ground.

Some motocross bikes are as loud as a jet plane coming in to land!

SUPER STATS

KTM 690 RALLY
TOP SPEED: 177 km/h (110+ mph)
WEIGHT: 162 kg (357 lbs)
ENGINE: 72 bhp
MADE IN: Austria
PRICE: Not for sale

ECOSSE TITANIUM SERIES

If superbikes are meant to be exotic, then the Ecosse Titanium may be the most super of all. This American-made speed machine has been constructed from some of the most expensive materials on earth. For a while, the Titanium was the costliest bike that money could buy. A newer version, called the FE Ti XX, sells for £192,000!

On the Ecosse even the exhaust pipe is made from titanium.

Titanium is a very difficult metal to weld, so extra care has been taken when making the Titanium series.

Each bike is individually numbered.

Titanium is a very expensive metal. Instead of painting it, Ecosse have hand-polished the titanium to show it off.

The suspension is up to Moto GP standard.

Although the Titaniums are amazing bikes, they are actually based on an older Ecosse model called the Heretic. This doesn't mean that the Titaniums have been easy to make. It actually took eighteen months of researching, designing and testing before the bikes were ready.

It's no surprise that the Titaniums are fast – the engines have been developed with a firm that builds drag bikes.

SUPER STATS

ECOSSE TITANIUM
TOP SPEED: Not known
WEIGHT: 200 kg (440 lbs)
ENGINE: 200+ bhp
MADE IN: USA
PRICE: £176,000

MOTO GP

The people who make motorbikes try lots of different ways of advertising their bikes. One popular way is through motorbike racing. Manufacturers hope that if their bikes do well in races, people may want to buy their machines. The two biggest forms of motorbike racing are called Moto GP and World Superbikes.

The engines of the bikes can be up to 800 cc. The cc stands for cubic capacity and shows the size of the cylinders.

Light, powerful bikes are very fast. Moto GP rules state that its bikes have to have a minimum weight of 150 kg (330 lbs).

The form of bike racing that is closest to Formula 1 car racing is called Moto GP. This is where the biggest bikes compete against each other. These aren't bikes that you can buy in any showroom. They are specially built just to compete in GP races and use the most up-to-date technology to make them as fast as possible.

Bikes like the Yamaha YZR-M1 are designed for race tracks and can't be ridden on public roads.

Riders lean forward into a streamlined position.

The Yamaha YZR-M1 has lightweight carbon brakes on the front wheels.

The wheels are made of magnesium, which is both light and strong.

SUPER STATS

YAMAHA YZR-M1
TOP SPEED: 320+ km/h (200+ mph)
WEIGHT: 150 kg (330 lbs)
ENGINE: 200+ bhp
MADE IN: Japan
PRICE: Not for sale

NCR M16

The wheels are made from carbon fibre, which is light and strong.

The engine covers are made from titanium.

The Italian bike firm NCR create custom-built dream machines – at a price many of us can only dream of. Each of their bikes is hand-made, with an attention to detail that would put watchmakers to shame. They are meant to be the world's most exclusive bikes.

The original steel frame has been replaced by a carbon fibre one.

The disc brakes on the wheels are ceramic rather than metal. Ceramic brakes do not overheat like metal ones.

All the aluminium used in the bike is of the same standard as that used in aircraft.

What NCR have done is take a replica Moto GP bike from another Italian bike manufacturer and make it even more amazing. The original bike was called the Ducatti Desmosedici RR. NCR have stripped it down and tuned it up. It's now a leaner, meaner, faster machine.

The M16 is only made on request.

The covers at the front of the bike are called fairings. The M16's fairings have been cut away to save weight.

The NCR has six gears.

SUPER STATS

NCR M16
TOP SPEED: Not released
WEIGHT: 145 kg (319 lbs)
ENGINE: 200+ bhp
MADE IN: Italy
PRICE: £100,000 (estimated) and £140,000 for the Ducatti Desmosedici RR

JAWA RACERS

Superbikes don't have to be jaw-droppingly powerful and expensive to give their riders maximum thrills. Some of the fastest bikes around are actually very basic. These lightweight machines compete in races where speed and nerves of steel go hand-in-hand.

Like all other speedway bikes, the Jawa has only one gear.

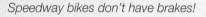
Speedway bikes don't have brakes!

One of the lightest, quickest racing bikes is the Jawa 889 speedway bike. Speedway racing sees four riders racing against each other round an oval track. The track is around 300 metres (984 ft) long and each four-lap race lasts for around a minute. The track surfaces are made from a loose material such as shale brick granules.

Jawa bikes also race in another competition that is very similar to speedway. There's just one major difference – the races take place on ice. The bikes used are like speedway bikes, but have some special modifications.

Ice racers have spiked tyres to get a better grip on the ice. The spikes are made from metal and screw into the tyres.

The Jawa accelerates to 100 km/h (62 mph) in about 3 seconds – that's nearly as fast as a Formula 1 race car.

The Jawa uses a fuel called methanol. This allows the engine to produce more power than petrol would.

SUPER STATS

JAWA 889
TOP SPEED: 110+ km/h (70+ mph)
WEIGHT: 80 kg (176 lbs)
ENGINE: 68 bhp
MADE IN: Czech Republic
PRICE: £4,600

MTT TURBINE SUPERBIKE

Superbike makers have tried lots of tricks to make their bikes go faster. New materials are used to make the bikes lighter. Different fuels have been tried to make the engines more powerful. But a manufacturer called MTT has done something remarkable. It has made a superbike with a completely different sort of engine – a turbine. Or what you and I would call a jet engine!

This is the fastest production bike in the world.

The turbine engine is made by Rolls Royce.

These fairings are made from carbon fibre.

The engine can run on diesel, kerosene or aviation fuel.

The Superbike once raced – and beat – a jet plane over a 1.6-km (one-mile) track.

MTT don't usually make bikes – they make custom-built, turbine-powered machines such as air boats and pumps. Turbine engines use high-speed compressed air and fuel to generate their power – and they can produce a lot of power. The engine in the MTT Superbike is often found in helicopters!

The frame of the Superbike is made from aluminium.

You've got to be patient to get your hands on one of these jet-powered marvels. They can take up to 12 weeks to build.

SUPER STATS

MTT TURBINE SUPERBIKE
TOP SPEED: 365 km/h (227 mph)
WEIGHT: 226 kg (500 lbs)
ENGINE: 320 bhp
MADE IN: USA
PRICE: £112,000

SUZUKI HAYABUSA

Many of the bikes in this book cost over £100,000 – and for that money, you'd expect something impressive. However, you don't have to spend that much to get a bike with a beast of an engine. One tenth of that cost will buy you a Suzuki Hayabusa – the most powerful production bike in the world.

The Hayabusa is blisteringly quick. It gets from 0-100 km/h (0-62 mph) in 2.7 seconds. It hits top speed in just over 18 seconds.

The Hayabusa's top speed is limited to 299 km/h (186 mph) for safety reasons. The bike could actually go quicker than this.

Hayabusas are famously reliable, and are known for not breaking down very often.

The world's fastest motorbike, the Ack Attack Streamliner (see pages 10-11) uses Hayabusa engines. That's how good they are!

The Suzuki Hayabusa has been in production since 1999. The name Hayabusa is actually Japanese for 'peregrine falcon'. It's a fitting name, as the peregrine is the fastest creature on the planet. It can reach speeds of over 322 km/h (200 mph) when it dives to catch its prey.

Two lights are better than one. The Hayabusa has twin headlights at the front, mounted one above the other.

The inside of the front suspension fork is coated with a diamond-like substance. This helps the inner tubes move up and down more smoothly.

SUPER STATS

SUZUKI HAYABUSA
TOP SPEED: 299 km/h (186 mph)
WEIGHT: 260 kg (573 lbs)
ENGINE: 194 bhp
MADE IN: Japan
PRICE: £10,935

HONDA GOLDWING

Not all superbikes are about brash displays of power and high-speed thrills. The Honda Goldwing's approach is more laid back and luxurious. Welcome to the world of the super touring bike. These massive machines are designed for long-distance driving – with supreme style and comfort.

Touring bikes need to store a rider's baggage. The Goldwing has around 150 litres of storage space with areas in the saddlebags, boot and fairings.

The Honda Goldwing is the king of the touring bike world. These iconic bikes have been in production since 1975. They are built for carrying a rider plus a passenger. Now the bikes come packed with more creature comforts than ever before.

There's no danger of getting lost – the Goldwing comes complete with a built-in satellite navigation system.

You can listen to music on touring bikes. The Goldwing has surround sound speakers and you can play either mp3s or cds.

Over 640,000 Honda Goldwings have been sold so far.

There are heated seats and warm air vents for your feet.

The seats are adjustable for both the rider and passenger.

Touring bikes are big and heavy, so they use lots of fuel. The Goldwing uses about the same amount of fuel as a family car.

SUPER STATS

**HONDA GL 1800
    GOLDWING DELUXE**

TOP SPEED: Not released
WEIGHT: 417 kg (919 lbs)
ENGINE: 118 bhp
MADE IN: Japan
PRICE: £23,125

HARLEY-DAVIDSON DYNA SUPER GLIDE CUSTOM

Some superbikes are good for one thing in particular – showing off. A good way of attracting attention is to customise your bike. This means adjusting the way it looks or rides. Manufacturers like Harley-Davidson will do all the hard work for you to create an eye-catching ride.

The Super Glide doesn't use modern metals such as titanium to get a shine. Instead it uses old-fashioned chrome – just like they used to.

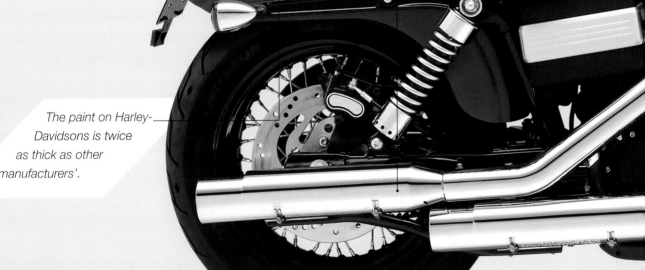

The paint on Harley-Davidsons is twice as thick as other manufacturers'.

Riders can customise their Super Glide in all sorts of ways. The suspension can be adjusted, different seats can be bought and even the engine can be altered.

Harley-Davidson is one of the most famous motorbike manufacturers in the world. This American company started building bikes in 1903 and was soon building iconic bikes that appealed to everyone from police forces to biker gangs. The Super Glide Custom is designed to look a little old fashioned to remind people of Harley's history.

The 'pullback' handlebars are comfortable to hold when cruising long distances.

All the gauges and instruments are positioned on the top of the fuel tank.

Customers can have anti-lock brakes if they want. These stop the wheels from locking if the bike slows down too quickly.

SUPER STATS

HARLEY-DAVIDSON DYNA SUPER GLIDE CUSTOM
TOP SPEED: 185 km/h (115 mph)
WEIGHT: 294 kg (648 lbs)
ENGINE: 65 bhp
MADE IN: USA
PRICE: From £8,330

REWACO FX6

If you want a superbike that really gets you noticed, you might need a completely different sort of machine. And nothing is more guaranteed to cause stares than a supertrike. Vehicles such as the Rewaco FX6 prove that three-wheelers aren't just for toddlers!

Customers can order a top box for storage and can also get saddlebags.

Stable, powerful trikes such as the Rewaco can even tow a trailer or caravan.

The engine is made by the famous American motorcycle firm, Harley-Davidson.

The FX6 has two seats, but up to four people can fit on some trikes.

The real advantage of trikes such as the Rewaco FX6 over bikes is that they are a lot more stable. Having three wheels means that you don't have to balance. So trike riders get all the feel and enjoyment of riding a motorbike – without the problem of falling off!

Lightness isn't really the top priority with the FX6, so there's lots of shiny chrome.

The FX6 might be heavy, but it can still get to 100 km/h (62 mph) in under 8 seconds!

The shock absorbers can be adjusted for a sporty or more comfortable ride.

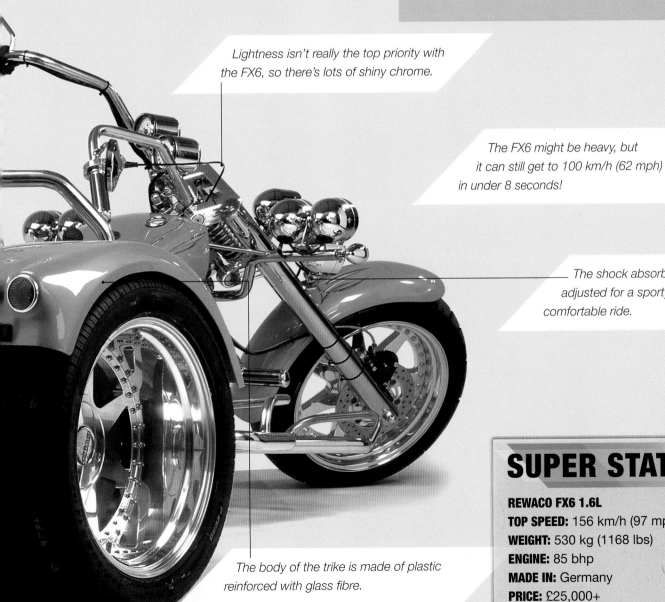

The body of the trike is made of plastic reinforced with glass fibre.

SUPER STATS

REWACO FX6 1.6L
TOP SPEED: 156 km/h (97 mph)
WEIGHT: 530 kg (1168 lbs)
ENGINE: 85 bhp
MADE IN: Germany
PRICE: £25,000+

SUPER

Some cars stand out from the crowd. They are faster, more expensive and better to drive than other cars. In short, they are supercars!

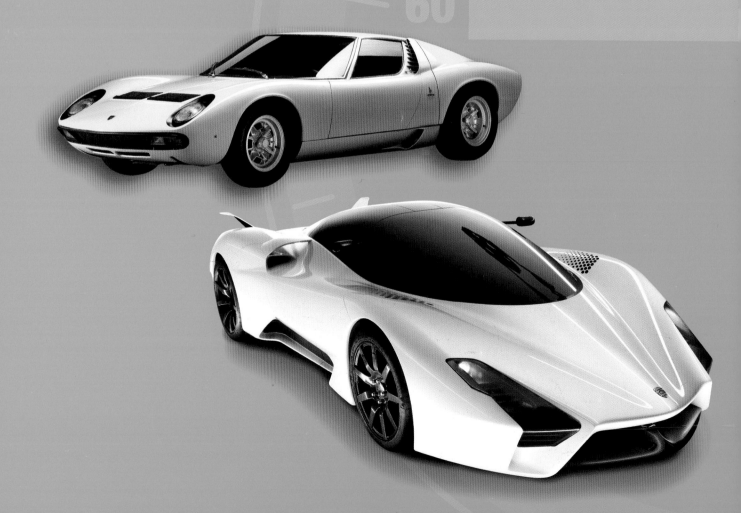

CARS

BUGATTI VEYRON SUPER SPORT

One of the sleekest supercars around is the Bugatti Veyron SSC but you'll need deep pockets to buy it. Only five Super Sports were made and they each sell for an incredible £1.4 million!

Nothing comes cheap on the Bugatti. An annual service at the garage will cost £26,000.

The body is made of carbon fibre, which is incredibly light but very strong.

Braking at high speed can cause normal brakes to fail. Cars like the Super Sport use brakes made of porcelain instead. Porcelain copes with heat better than metal brakes.

The speed has been restricted on road-going models to 415 km/h (258 mph) in order to save the tyres from being destroyed. As it costs £17,300 for a set of tyres, this is probably a good idea.

What makes the Bugatti Veyron SSC a supercar? For a start it is the fastest production car in the world. It can accelerate to 100 km/h (62 mph) in 2.5 seconds and has an incredible top speed of nearly 421km/h (262 mph)!

A wing pops out of the back of the car when it reaches 182 km/h (113 mph). The wing uses the wind to push the car down to help it grip the road.

The powerful engine was designed for speed and not fuel economy. The Super Sport does a measly 37 litres per 100 km (7.6 miles per gallon) when driving around town.

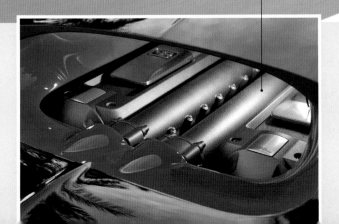

SUPER STATS

BUGATTI VEYRON SUPER SPORT
TOP SPEED: 420.998 km/h (267.81 mph)
0-100 KM/H (0-62MPH): 2.5 seconds
FUEL ECONOMY (COMBINED):
   23.15 l/100 km (12.2 miles per gallon)
HORSEPOWER: 1183 bhp
LENGTH: 4462 mm (175.6 in)
WIDTH: 1998 mm (78.6 in)
HEIGHT: 1204 mm (47.4 in)
MADE IN: Germany
PRICE: £1.4 million

FORMULA ONE

If you love high-speed thrills and spills, then car racing is the place to be. The world's fastest, most pulse-pounding motorsports are Formula One and drag racing.

Big wheels give lots of grip.

Wings at the front and back of the car use the wind to help push the car down onto the track to improve grip.

Formula One is the most expensive and glamorous of all motorsports.
These cars have powerful engines and lightweight bodies for tearing around tracks at high speed. Strict rules control what racing teams can do to their cars. Engineers try to find ways of making their cars even faster within these rules.

DRAG RACING

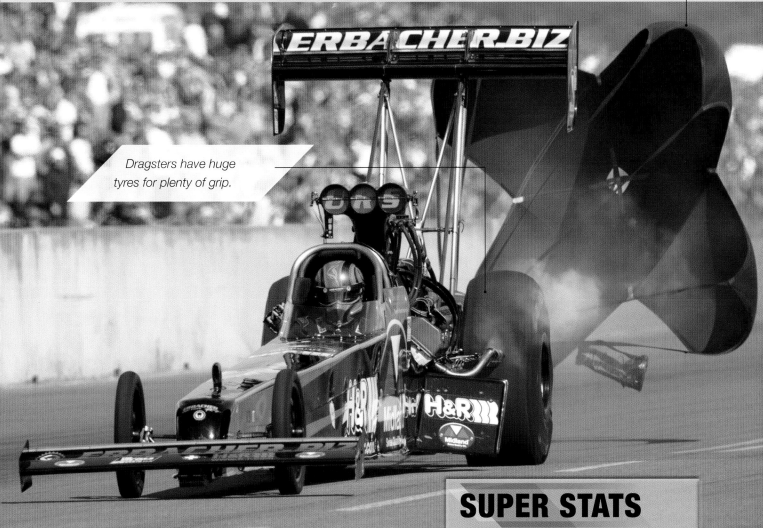

Dragsters need parachutes to help them slow down.

Dragsters have huge tyres for plenty of grip.

Formula One may be quick, but drag racing is quicker. These cars sprint down a straight, 400-m- (quarter-mile-) long track. They rocket along at over 531 km/h (330 mph). Dragsters have small, light front wheels and big rear wheels. Their engines run on a special fuel called nitro-methane.

SUPER STATS

RED BULL F1 CAR (OPPOSITE)

TOP SPEED: top secret, but over 320 km/h (200 mph)

0-100 KM/H (0-62MPH): top secret (but estimated at around 2.5 seconds)

FUEL ECONOMY (ESTIMATED): 70.6 l/100 km (4 mpg)

HORSEPOWER: top secret (estimated at over 700 bhp)

LENGTH (ESTIMATED): 4635 mm (182.4 in)

WIDTH (ESTIMATED): 1800 mm (70.8 in)

HEIGHT (ESTIMATED): 950 mm (37.4 in)

MADE IN: Austria

PRICE: not for sale

THRUST SSC

No car on Earth is faster — or rarer – than Thrust SSC. This one-off wonder holds the land speed record. That means that it's not just the fastest thing on four wheels. It's the fastest thing on any number of wheels, legs... or even skis!

A normal car engine – even one from a supercar – couldn't hope to get Thrust to anywhere near its top speed. So engineers gave Thrust something different – two jet engines!

Thrust's driver was an ex-airforce pilot called Andy Green. At least he was used to the speed!

The engines are the same as those used on Phantom jet fighters.

The wheels are made from metal. There are no tyres – they would fall apart at these high speeds.

Thrust SSC set the land speed record on October 15, 1997. The attempt took place at Black Rock Desert, Arizona, USA. For a record to be official the car has to do two runs over a distance of 1.6 km (a mile). The average speed of the two runs is taken. The average Thrust SSC achieved was a phenomenal 1227.985 km/h (763.035 mph)!

Many land speed record attempts happen in deserts like Black Rock. They are flat and dry – perfect conditions for speedy driving.

The engines sit either side of the driver's cabin.

The engines run on aviation fuel, the same stuff that powers jet planes.

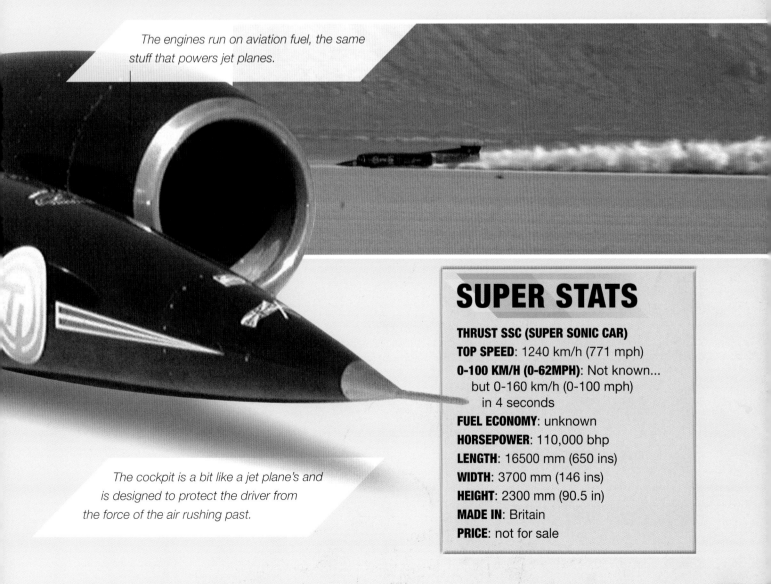

The cockpit is a bit like a jet plane's and is designed to protect the driver from the force of the air rushing past.

SUPER STATS

THRUST SSC (SUPER SONIC CAR)
TOP SPEED: 1240 km/h (771 mph)
0-100 KM/H (0-62MPH): Not known... but 0-160 km/h (0-100 mph) in 4 seconds
FUEL ECONOMY: unknown
HORSEPOWER: 110,000 bhp
LENGTH: 16500 mm (650 ins)
WIDTH: 3700 mm (146 ins)
HEIGHT: 2300 mm (90.5 in)
MADE IN: Britain
PRICE: not for sale

LAMBORGHINI MIURA

The Lamborghini Miura was first built in 1968. It became an instant classic and these days many experts call it the world's first supercar. Why? Because it was stunningly beautiful, shockingly fast and the engineering was very advanced for its time.

The radiator, fans and spare wheel are under the bonnet.

The headlamps rise up by roughly 30 degrees when switched on.

Marcello Gandini designed the bodywork. It was the first car he worked on – before that he had designed the insides of nightclubs!

Lamborghini started out making tractors, not cars – though farmers have never travelled as fast as this.

Like many supercars, the Miura is not very practical. It has little boot space, the cabin is cramped, it's difficult to park, and you can hardly see out of the back. But – and it's a big but – it is also one of the most thrilling cars you can possibly drive. And that's what supercars are all about.

The engine is placed as near to the middle of the car as possible to help the Miura stay balanced. Only racing cars had done this in the past.

The boot is a small space left behind the engine.

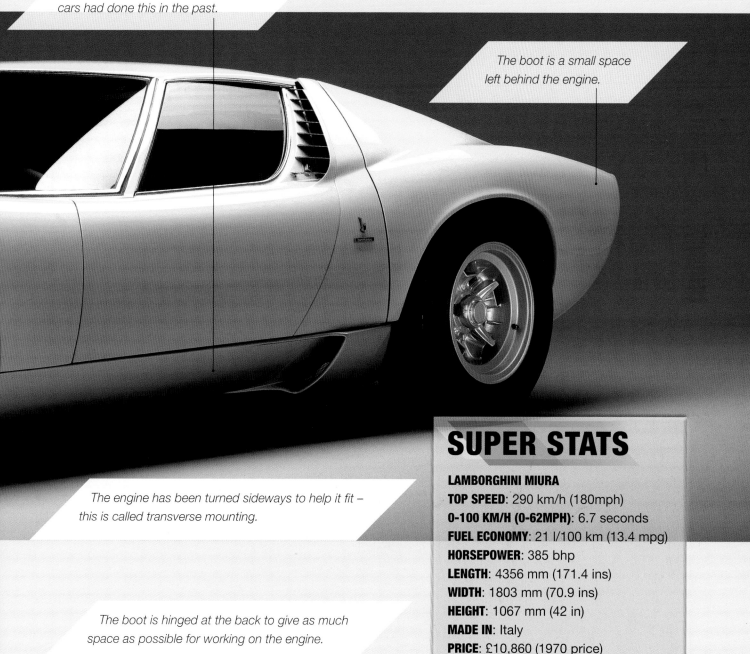

The engine has been turned sideways to help it fit – this is called transverse mounting.

The boot is hinged at the back to give as much space as possible for working on the engine.

SUPER STATS

LAMBORGHINI MIURA
TOP SPEED: 290 km/h (180mph)
0-100 KM/H (0-62MPH): 6.7 seconds
FUEL ECONOMY: 21 l/100 km (13.4 mpg)
HORSEPOWER: 385 bhp
LENGTH: 4356 mm (171.4 ins)
WIDTH: 1803 mm (70.9 ins)
HEIGHT: 1067 mm (42 in)
MADE IN: Italy
PRICE: £10,860 (1970 price)

FERRARI 599 GTB

The Italian car firm Ferrari is perhaps the most famous of all the supercar makers. They started building racing cars in the 1940s, and by 1948 they also made road versions of these cars. The Ferrari symbol of a black horse goes hand in hand with the best supercars money can buy.

Lightweight aluminium body

HF07 CUV

The technology from Ferrari's Formula One racing cars is often found in their road cars. The Ferrari 599 is a good example of this. The driver changes gear by pressing paddles on the steering wheel. A computer helps to manage how the car handles on the road and how the suspension works. These ideas were both trialled in Formula One.

Inside, the cabin uses leather, aluminium and carbon fibre for a lightweight but luxurious feel.

The 599 GTB is called a grand tourer. These cars are designed to travel long distances in style and comfort – and at speed! Unfortunately, because of their terrible fuel consumption, you'll need a hefty salary to travel far in a car like this.

Carbon fibre brakes

The rear tyres are 2.5 cm (0.98 in) bigger than the front tyres.

SUPER STATS

FERRARI 599 GTB
TOP SPEED: Over 330 km/h (205 mph)
0-100 KM/H (0-62MPH): 3.7 seconds
FUEL ECONOMY: 21.2 l/100 km (13.3 mpg)
HORSEPOWER: 612 bhp
LENGTH: 4666 mm (183.7 in)
WIDTH: 1960 mm (77.2 in)
HEIGHT: 1336 mm (52.6 in)
MADE IN: Italy
PRICE: £177,325

ROLLS ROYCE
PHANTOM

Sometimes speed alone isn't enough. If you become a millionaire (good luck with that!), you might want something not just super-fast, but also super-luxurious. The Rolls Royce Phantom is one of the most luxurious supercars in the world.

The Phantom comes in 16 different colours. If you are willing to pay extra, Rolls Royce will make it any colour you like.

Rolls Royce cars have a small metal statue of a woman at the front. She is called the Spirit of Ecstasy.

The design of the radiator grill is the same on all Rolls Royces.

The wheels are half the height of the car. This is thought to be the best ratio for a good-looking car.

If buyers want more leg room in the back, they can get an extended version of the car, which is 250 mm (9.8 in) longer.

Rolls Royce is one of the most famous names in the motoring world. The company was founded in 1904. Rolls Royce pride themselves on making the most comfortable and quiet cars around. In the past, most Rolls Royce owners would have had chauffeurs. Today, the cars are so much fun to drive that most owners wouldn't let anyone else behind the wheel.

Around 55 metres (180 ft) of leather is used in the inside of the car.

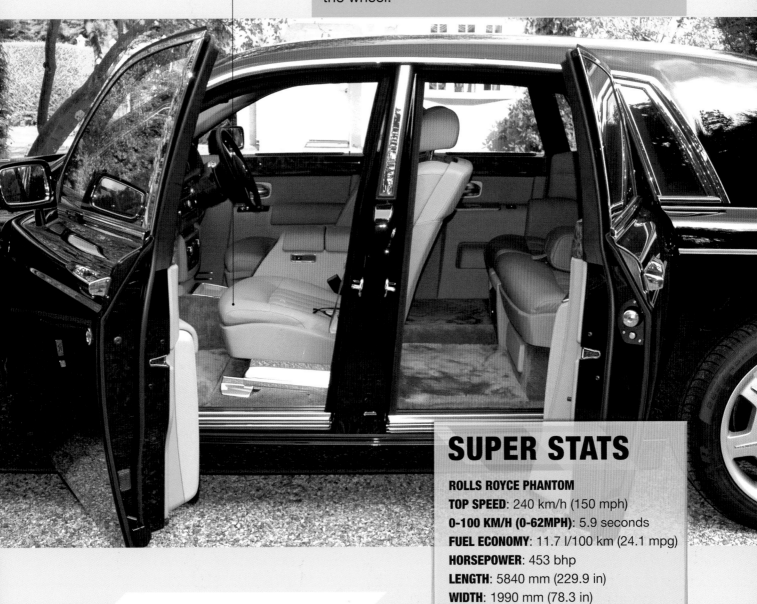

The frame is made from lightweight aluminium. Lightness is important even on big cars like the Phantom.

SUPER STATS

ROLLS ROYCE PHANTOM
TOP SPEED: 240 km/h (150 mph)
0-100 KM/H (0-62MPH): 5.9 seconds
FUEL ECONOMY: 11.7 l/100 km (24.1 mpg)
HORSEPOWER: 453 bhp
LENGTH: 5840 mm (229.9 in)
WIDTH: 1990 mm (78.3 in)
HEIGHT: 1638 mm (64.5 in)
MADE IN: Britain
PRICE: £285,200

MERCEDES SLS AMG

German company Mercedes-Benz has a very special place in motoring history. In 1885, Karl Benz built the world's first petrol-powered motor car. Today his company is still ahead of the game and produces cars like the breathtaking SLS AMG.

The odd-looking doors are called gullwings. They look cool, but gullwing doors can be awkward to close, and if you park too close to something else, you're going to hit it.

197 MBC

The SLS is the perfect combination of old and new. Its name and design hark back to the 1950s. However, its engineering is cutting edge. The engine has been tuned to be as powerful and as fast as possible.

The weight of the car is almost perfectly balanced between the front and back. A well-balanced car should handle better.

When the 300 SL was built in 1954, its makers claimed that it was the fastest road car in the world. It was also the first to use gull-wing doors. It had these unusual doors because the shape of the body and the way it was made meant normal doors wouldn't fit.

The chassis and the body are made from lightweight aluminium, to keep the weight down.

SUPER STATS

MERCEDES SLS AMG
TOP SPEED: 317 km/h (197 mph)
0-100 KM/H (0-62MPH): 3.8 seconds
FUEL ECONOMY: 13.2 l/100 km (21.4 mpg)
HORSEPOWER: 571 bhp
LENGTH: 4638 mm (182.5 in)
WIDTH: 1939 mm (76.3 in)
HEIGHT: 1260 mm (49.6 in)
MADE IN: Germany
PRICE: £168,395

XENATEC MAYBACH COUPE

In the world of the supercar, there's no limit to how much cars can be modified. Engines can be tuned to make them more powerful. The interior and even the chassis can be transformed too. That's exactly what has happened with the Xenatec Maybach Coupe.

Customers can have a glass roof instead of the standard steel one if they want.

The inside of the car has thicker carpet than most people's houses.

The original car that Xenatec modifies is a Maybach 57S. Maybach is the luxury brand belonging to Mercedes Benz.

The angles of the windscreen and rear windows have been altered. Also, the pillars at the rear of the car have been moved further back to make getting in and out easier.

German company Xenatec specialises in altering other manufacturers' cars. The Maybach coupe starts life as an already luxurious saloon from another company, called Maybach. Xenatec then makes it a little bit more special. The basic mechanics of the car stay the same, but the interior and exterior get a make-over.

Most of the exterior panels are different from those of the original car. Even the bumpers have been changed.

The original Maybach car has four doors but Xenatec rebuilds the body to make a sportier-looking two door coupe.

SUPER STATS

XENATEC MAYBACH COUPE
TOP SPEED: 275 km/h (171 mph)
0-100 KM/H (0-62MPH): 4.9 seconds
FUEL ECONOMY: 19 l/100km (14.8 mpg)
HORSEPOWER: 603 bhp
LENGTH: 5728 mm (225.5 in)
WIDTH: 1980 mm (77.9 in)
HEIGHT: 1544 mm (60.7 in)
MADE IN: Germany
PRICE: £285,200

PAGANI ZONDA R

Some companies can never be satisfied in their quest for speed. The Pagani Zonda was one of the fastest and most fun-to-drive cars in the world. However, the perfectionists at Pagani obviously decided that it wasn't quite fast enough or fun enough – so they invented the Zonda R.

A big air scoop on the roof forces the wind over the engine to help keep it cool.

The tyres are slick, which means they have no tread. These give more grip – unless it's raining, and then they are useless.

The suspension makes the ride smoother. On the Zonda R this can be adjusted to suit each individual driver.

The Zonda R was created for belting around a race track at blistering speeds. Racing circuits and test tracks sometimes allow sports car owners to bring their own vehicles along to give them a spin. The appeal is that you can drive your car at speeds way beyond those allowed on the roads.

Most of the car is made from either carbon or titanium – including the chassis. Carbon and titanium are both light and strong.

The wing can be adjusted to give more or less downforce.

The tyres were made especially for this car by tyre company Pirelli.

The engines are made by Mercedes Benz and have been tuned by AMG. The same engines have been used by Mercedes – in a racing car!

SUPER STATS

PAGANI ZONDA R
TOP SPEED: 275 km/h (171 mph)
0-100 KM/H (0-62MPH): 2.7 seconds
FUEL ECONOMY: not known
HORSEPOWER: 750 bhp
LENGTH: 4866 mm (191.5 in)
WIDTH: 2014 mm (79.2 in)
HEIGHT: 1141 mm (44.9 in)
MADE IN: Italy
PRICE: £1.2 million (estimated)

SHELBY TUATARA

When the Bugatti Veyron Super Sport became the world's fastest car, it took the crown from a small American company, Shelby Super Cars, and their SSC Ultimate Aero. Now Shelby wants the record back. This is the car they've built to do it: the Shelby Tuatara.

The body is made of carbon fibre.

The odd-looking winglets help provide downforce.

Even the wheels are made from carbon fibre.

Many of the details of the Tuatara have been kept top secret. We do know that the Tuatara will use the classic combination of power and lightness in its record attempt. The engine produces a staggering 1,350 bhp, and the car itself is mostly made from lightweight carbon fibre. Is it enough to beat the Veyron Super Sport? Only time will tell.

Added strength comes from metal crash supports. These will protect the car in any high-speed accidents.

The Tuatara is designed to be as aerodynamic as possible. This means that the air slips around the car when it moves. The more easily a car moves through the air, the faster it goes.

Grooves underneath the car use the passing air to help the car grip the road.

Big air scoops at the front, side and rear of the car will cool the engine and create downforce.

SUPER STATS

SHELBY TUATARA

TOP SPEED: 442 km/h (275 mph) estimated

0-100 KM/H (0-62MPH): 2.8 seconds estimated

FUEL ECONOMY: not known

HORSEPOWER: 1350 bhp

LENGTH: not known

WIDTH: not known

HEIGHT: not known

MADE IN: USA

PRICE: not known

BOWLER NEMESIS

Not all supercars are for tearing around race tracks or cruising around town. Some of them are designed to go places where normal machines fear to drive – such as off-road in deserts or forests. No car does this better than the Bowler Nemesis.

The Nemesis is wide and squat, but with plenty of space between the ground and the bottom of the car – perfect for off-roading.

The tyres are big, chunky and ideal for getting a grip on wet or slippery surfaces.

The Nemesis isn't any old off-roader. It is designed for high-speed, off-road racing. This takes it through some of the most difficult terrain in the world. You need a real supercar to compete in that, along with some pretty extraordinary modifications such as hydraulic rams, sand ladders and fire extinguishers.

The Nemesis was designed to compete in the Dakar Rally. This race used to go from Paris, France to Dakar, Senegal. In the last few years the race has been held in South America instead.

The body is made from carbon fibre and a material called Twin-tex.

An internal cage protects the driver if the Nemesis rolls over.

The boot contains three spare wheels, sand ladders, tools, shovels, first-aid equipment and spare water. You don't need all that going to the shops!

The car has a hydraulic ram fitted underneath. This is like a jack that pushes the car up off the ground if it gets stuck in the sand.

SUPER STATS

BOWLER NEMESIS
TOP SPEED: 225 km/h (140 mph)
0-100 KM/H (0-62MPH): 5 seconds
FUEL ECONOMY: not known
HORSEPOWER: 257 bhp
LENGTH: 4436 mm (174.6 in)
WIDTH: 2000 mm (78.7 in)
HEIGHT: 1730 mm (68.1 in)
MADE IN: Britain
PRICE: £164,220

NISSAN GT-R

Supercars don't have to be expensive – they just have to be special. Like its more costly rivals, the Nissan GTR looks remarkable. And it really is fast. The only difference between the GTR and most other supercars is that it can be yours for around half the price of the competition.

The GTR is a practical supercar. It has a big boot and could easily carry home a family's supermarket shop.

The Japanese-built GTR may be cheaper than its European rivals. However, it's more than a match for them on the track. The GTR has excellent road-handling, a 0-100 time of just over 3 seconds and a top speed of 315 km/h (196 mph). There's not much that would beat it around a race track.

The Nissan GTR has four-wheel drive. This means that the engine powers all four wheels. Usually car engines only power two of the wheels.

Brembo fully ventilated drilled steel disc brakes

Independent Transaxle 4WD
GR6-type dual clutch transmission

Multi-structured body

VR38-type twin turbo engine

Bilstein DampTronic dampers

Large-diameter run-flat tires

GT R

Premium Midship Package

'Run flat' tyres can still be used even if they get a puncture.

The GTR's mighty engine has won it the nickname 'Godzilla'.

Scoops and vents in the bonnet help to cool the engine.

There's no getting lost in the dark with these super-bright xenon headlights.

The tyres are filled with a gas called nitrogen instead of air. Air expands when it heats up, but nitrogen doesn't. This way the tyres don't get bigger while driving fast.

SUPER STATS

NISSAN GT-R
TOP SPEED: 315 km/h (196 mph)
0-100 KM/H (0-62MPH): 3.046 seconds
FUEL ECONOMY: 12 l/100 km (23.5 mpg)
HORSEPOWER: 523 bhp
LENGTH: 4650 mm (183 in)
WIDTH: 1895 mm (74.6 in)
HEIGHT: 1370 mm (53.9 in)
MADE IN: Japan
PRICE: £71,950

KOENIGSEGG AGERA R

Perhaps the biggest problem with supercars is the effect they have on the environment. Supercars use a lot of fuel. This results in exhaust gases that can help cause climate change. However, the Agera R is different – it uses biofuels, which produce fewer harmful gases. Now you can have a supercar and a clear conscience.

The tyres are designed to cope with speeds of up to 420 km/h (260 mph).

The roof panel can be removed for open-top motoring.

The wheels are designed to generate more downforce from the wind.

Super-fast cars need incredible brakes. The Agera R accelerates from 0 to 322 km/h (200 mph) and back in just under 25 seconds.

The Agera R doesn't just look amazing. There's lots of clever engineering here too. The car is made of carbon fibre and aluminium to keep it light for speed. Fast, light cars need lots of grip. The Agera gets its grip from smart use of wind, exhaust gases and special wheels that create downforce.

The angle of the rear wing changes depending on how fast the air moves over it, for maximum effect.

Exhaust gases come out of vents in the rear pylons, which increase downforce.

The Agera R can run on petrol, as well as biofuels.

The body is partly made from Kevlar – the same material that is used in bullet-proof vests.

SUPER STATS

KOENIGSEGG AGERA R
TOP SPEED: 418+ km/h (260+ mph)
0-100 KM/H (0-62MPH): 2.9 seconds
FUEL ECONOMY: 12 l/100 km (23.5 mpg)
HORSEPOWER: 1115 bhp
LENGTH: 4293 mm (169 ins)
WIDTH: 1996 mm (78.6 ins)
HEIGHT: 1129 mm (44.5 ins)
MADE IN: Sweden
PRICE: £1,000,000+ (estimated)

TESLA ROADSTER SPORT

In the past, the only road vehicle that put no exhaust gases into the air was a bicycle. Electric vehicles changed that, but they were slow and the batteries that provided the power ran out after just a few miles. Then came the Tesla Roadster: a supercar for the green generation.

The roadster gets its power from 6831 lithium-ion batteries.

The batteries are rechargeable. You just plug the car in to charge it up.

The Tesla Roadster has everything you could want from a supercar. One thing is missing though: there's no engine noise. In common with all electric cars, the Roadster is as quiet as a mouse's sigh. The only noises you hear are the tyres on the road and the wind rushing by.

The batteries charge each time the driver brakes, too.

Batteries last for seven years and have a range of 394 km (245 miles) between charges.

Batteries are stacked behind the seats.

Electric cars might be green but they do have problems. It can take 13 hours to recharge the Roadster from a normal plug. This means journeys of over 394 km (245 miles) are out of the question.

The body is hand made from carbon fibre panels.

Wheels are made from aluminium.

SUPER STATS

TESLA ROADSTER SPORT
TOP SPEED: 201 km/h (125 mph)
0-100 KM/H (0-62MPH): 3.7 seconds
FUEL ECONOMY: does not apply
HORSEPOWER: 288 bhp
LENGTH: 3939.5 mm (155.1 ins)
WIDTH: 1851.6 mm (72.9 ins)
HEIGHT: 1126.5 mm (44.35 ins)
MADE IN: USA
PRICE: £90,000

SUPER

Planes are the kings of the sky. No other vehicles (apart from spacecraft) can match them for soaring elegance and blistering speed. This chapter is about the most amazing aircraft: the superplanes.

PLANES

X-43A

The most 'super' of all the mega flying machines is the incredible X-43A. It has set many airspeed records for jet-propelled aircraft, making it the fastest plane on Earth.

The X-43A takes a piggyback on another plane.

When the plane reaches 12,000 m (40,000 ft), the booster unit is set free.

The X-43A, which is mounted at the front end of the booster unit, is released when it reaches around 27,500 m (90,000 ft).

The X-43A is made by NASA, the American organisation in charge of space exploration. It has no room for passengers – or even a pilot. Each X-43A lasts for just one flight, before it is deliberately crashed. It is an experimental plane, and is used to test out new technology and ideas about flight.

The X-43A uses a type of engine called a scramjet. This uses fast-moving air mixed with hydrogen fuel to provide the power.

Its top speed is a remarkable Mach 9.6, which is nearly 11,200 km/h (7,000 mph).

SUPER STATS

X-43A

LENGTH: 3.7 m (12 ft)
WINGSPAN: 1.5 m (5 ft)
RANGE: (estimated) 1450 km (900 miles)
NUMBER OF CREW: 0
NUMBER OF PASSENGERS: 0
TOP SPEED: Mach 9.6

VIRGIN ATLANTIC GLOBALFLYER

Today it's possible for planes to fly right around the world without landing. The trick is to stay in the air with the least fuel possible. The GlobalFlyer was designed and built with one purpose in mind – to beat the record for the distance covered by a plane without refuelling.

At 35 m (114 ft), GlobalFlyer's wings are as wide as a passenger jet airliner.

Remarkably, GlobalFlyer has just one jet engine.

The wings are made from carbon fibre, which is both very light and very strong.

Breaking the distance record in 2005 meant travelling right the way around the world non-stop. And this is exactly what pilot Steve Fosset managed in 76 hours, 42 minutes and 55 seconds. In 2006, he flew even further. The 2006 journey took GlobalFlyer from Florida, USA, all the way around the world and then onwards to Bournemouth, Great Britain.

The plane needs parachutes to slow it down when coming in to land.

GlobalFlyer has 13 fuel tanks, which together hold 8,480 kg (18,700 lbs) of fuel.

SUPER STATS

VIRGIN ATLANTIC GLOBALFLYER
LENGTH: 11.8 m (38 ft 6 ins)
WINGSPAN: 35 m (114 ft)
RANGE: (estimated) 41,657 km (25,884 miles)
NUMBER OF CREW: 1
NUMBER OF PASSENGERS: 0
TOP SPEED: 550.8 km/h (342.24 mph)

NORTHROP GRUMMAN B-2 SPIRIT

Advances in technology are often driven by the military. The B-2 Spirit is an extraordinary warplane belonging to the United States Air Force. It's often called the 'stealth bomber'. It's one of the most advanced superplanes in existence.

The shape of the B-2 is called a 'flying wing'. This means the front edges of wings are angled at 33° and the rear of the wing is in a "w" shape.

The B-2 can fly around 9,600 km (6,000 miles) without being refuelled.

Refuelling can happen in mid-air! This gives the B-2 an overall range of around 16,000 km (10,000 miles).

The height a plane travels above sea level is called its altitude. The B-2 can fly at a maximum altitude of 15,200 m (50,000 ft).

The military are normally able to track planes using radar. However, the B-2 Spirit is incredibly difficult to detect. The shape of the plane, the amount of noise it makes and even the type of paint used on it make it almost impossible to spot. This is good news for the pilot – if nobody can see you, nobody can try to shoot at you!

The B-2's long range means it can fly anywhere in the world from its base in the USA.

SUPER STATS

NORTHROP GRUMMAN B-2 SPIRIT
LENGTH: 20.9 m (69 ft)
WINGSPAN: 52.12 m (171 ft)
RANGE: (without refuelling) 9,600 km (6,000 miles)
NUMBER OF CREW: 2
NUMBER OF PASSENGERS: 0
TOP SPEED: top secret

All this technology does not come cheap. Each B-2 costs a staggering £1.4 billion!

LOCKHEED SR-71 BLACKBIRD

Countries across the globe use spy planes to keep an eye on what their enemies are up to. One of the most successful spy planes ever was the SR-71, nicknamed 'Blackbird'. The idea behind the Blackbird was simple – it would travel really high and really quickly.

Blackbird flew from New York to London in just under 1 hour 55 minutes. Modern day passenger jets take around seven hours!

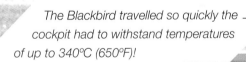

The Blackbird travelled so quickly the cockpit had to withstand temperatures of up to 340ºC (650ºF)!

Blackbird could travel higher and faster than enemy missiles so it couldn't be shot down!

Blackbird was used by the United States Air Force. It entered service in 1966 and was officially retired in 1998. Blackbird set many flying records. It is still the plane that could fly the highest in level flight. It's also the fastest standard jet plane.

The Blackbird could fly at altitudes of over 25,900 m (85,000 ft).

SUPER STATS

LOCKHEED SR-71 BLACKBIRD
LENGTH: 16.9 m (55 ft 7 ins)
WINGSPAN: 32.7 m (107 ft 3 ins)
RANGE: 4,660+ km (2,900+ miles)
NUMBER OF CREW: 2
NUMBER OF PASSENGERS: 0
TOP SPEED: 3,530 km/h (2,193 mph)

ANTONOV AN-225 MRIYA

The Antonov AN-225 Mriya is a transport plane – but it's no ordinary cargo carrier. The Mriya, which first flew in 1998, is the biggest plane in the world. It can carry cargo weighing up to 250,000 kg (550,000 lbs). There's enough space to hold 50 cars, or the fuselage (body) of a Boeing 737 airliner.

The Mriya is so heavy that it has to spread its weight across an amazing 32 wheels.

The Mriya is large enough — not to mention powerful enough — to carry a spacecraft on its back.

Mriya is Ukrainian for 'dream'. It was designed to give a piggyback to Buran, Russia's version of the Space Shuttle. While Buran was being tested, it hitched a ride on top of the Mriya. Buran was not a success and the project was abandoned. However, Mriya survived, and is still flying today.

The Mriya needs an airstrip 3.5 km (2.175 miles) long in order to take off when fully loaded.

A massive plane needs a lot of power to get it airborne. That's why Mriya has six engines.

The front of the plane lifts up to reveal the cargo-holding area.

SUPER STATS

ANTONOV AN-225 MRIYA
LENGTH: 84 m (275 ft 6 ins)
WINGSPAN: 88.4 m (290 ft)
RANGE: (unloaded) 14,000 km (8,699 miles)
NUMBER OF CREW: 6
NUMBER OF PASSENGERS: 0
TOP SPEED: 850 km/h (528 mph)

AIRBUS A380-800

The world's biggest passenger airliner is the Airbus A380-800. It's one of the most modern planes too, using new materials and greener engines to prove it's a real superplane.

The A380 uses less fuel per passenger than any other airliner – which is good news for the environment.

A big plane needs lots of paint, and the A380 has three coats. The paint alone weighs 500 kg (1,102 lbs)!

More people fly these days than ever before. Plane passengers made 2.75 billion trips in 2011. Busier airports lead to more flights and more fuel being used and more damage to the environment. The answer to the problem might be having bigger planes that use less fuel – planes like the Airbus A380.

The A380 is the world's only completely double-decker plane.

Airlines can decide on how many seats their A380s have. The numbers range from 525 up to 853! No other plane can carry more passengers.

There are 220 windows.

The A380 has quieter engines than other big airliners.

SUPER STATS

AIRBUS A380-800
LENGTH: 72.72 m (239 ft)
WINGSPAN: 79.75 m (261 ft)
RANGE: 15, 400 km (9,570 miles)
NUMBER OF CREW: 2 (plus flight attendants)
NUMBER OF PASSENGERS: 853
TOP SPEED: 1090 km/h (677 mph)

GULFSTREAM G650

How do the world's most glamorous celebrities, most powerful politicians and richest tycoons glide from one place to another in complete luxury? They travel by private jet. One of the most luxurious of private jets is the Gulfstream G650.

The turned-up parts at the end of each wing are called winglets. They are like extensions to the wings.

There are twelve different ways of arranging the seating. If none of those are to your liking, you can get a custom-made layout instead!

Even the air inside the G650 is better than in a large passenger jet. It's kept 100% fresh, unlike the recycled air in big planes.

This superplane is bigger, faster and quieter than most of its rivals. Now that's the way to travel! However, you need deep pockets to own a private jet. A G650 will cost you from around £36 million!

Two Rolls Royce engines provide the power. They have been designed to make less noise than the engines of most private jets.

The cabin interior is 1.95 m (6 ft 5 ins) high – that's high enough for people to walk around.

SUPER STATS

GULFSTREAM G650
LENGTH: 30.4 m (99 ft 9 ins)
WINGSPAN: 28.55 m (93 ft 8 ins)
RANGE: 12,964 km (8,055 miles)
NUMBER OF CREW: 2 (and 2 flight attendants if required)
NUMBER OF PASSENGERS: 18
TOP SPEED: 1,133 km/h (704 mph)

DORNIER CD2 SEASTAR

Aircraft need runways to land on – and the bigger the plane, the longer the runway. However, this is not the case with seaplanes. These are a weird cross between boats and aircraft. They are sometimes called flying boats.

Propellers at the back push the plane through the air. Propellers at the front pull the plane forwards.

The Seastar can land on either land or water.

With its boat-like design, the Seastar is happy to spend all its down time on the water.

The Seastar has two engines, one right behind the other. These are called in-line engines.

Seaplanes have been flown for over 100 years. These days seaplanes are often light aircraft that have been converted to land on the water. This is not the case with the Dornier CD2 Seastar. This is the first specially built ocean-going seaplane for over 50 years.

The design of the inside of the Seastar can be changed, so the plane can be used to carry cargo or even work as a flying ambulance.

The Seastar's fuselage (body) is made of materials that won't rust.

The passenger area can be arranged with either 12 or 9 seats, or as a more luxurious six-seater with more leg room.

SUPER STATS

DORNIER CD2 SEASTAR
LENGTH: 12. 67 m (41 ft 7 ins)
WINGSPAN: 17.71 m (58 ft 2 ins)
RANGE: 1,574.2 km (978 miles)
NUMBER OF CREW: 2 (though just 1 pilot is required)
NUMBER OF PASSENGERS: 12
TOP SPEED: 333 km/h (207 mph)

EDGLEY OPTICA

Sometimes it can be handy to get a bird's eye view of a situation. For example, you might want to keep an eye on traffic, or search for things on the ground. Normal planes travel too fast to get a good look. However, the Edgley Optica is a very different kind of plane.

The Optica is one of the quietest planes around.

The Optica has three seats, so it can be used as a sight-seeing plane for tourist trips.

The Edgley Optica was designed to be good at flying at low speeds. This means it's great for observing what's going on below. As a small propeller-driven plane, the Optica is much cheaper to run than a helicopter.

The cockpit of the plane is in front of the fan to give the passengers a clear view. The pilot and passenger can see 270° around them.

The plane is powered through the air by a ducted fan. This is a short propeller sitting inside a round case.

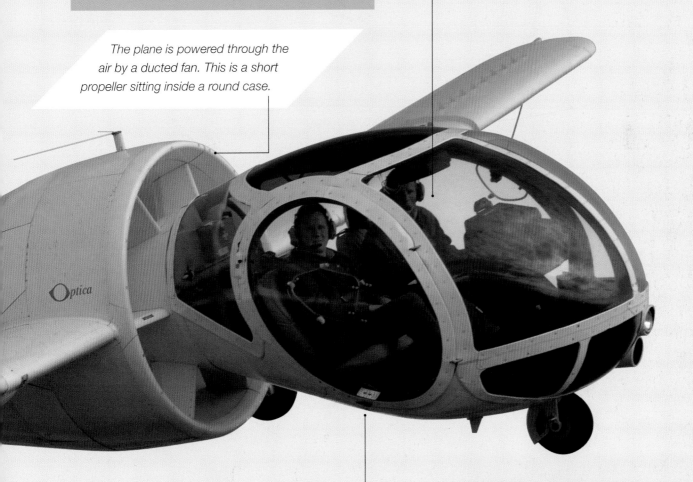

There's even glass on the floor, so the passengers can see what is below.

SUPER STATS

EDGLEY OPTICA
LENGTH: 8.1 m (26 ft 6 ins)
WINGSPAN: 12 m (39 ft 4 ins)
RANGE: 1055 km (656 miles)
NUMBER OF CREW: 1
NUMBER OF PASSENGERS: 2
TOP SPEED: 212 km/h (132 mph)

BOMBARDIER 415

Some superplanes do much more than travelling fast, or carrying heavy loads. These superplanes save lives. The Bombardier 415 is a fire-fighting seaplane. It is specially designed to tackle forest fires in areas that wheeled vehicles can't get to.

This is the only aircraft designed for aerial fire-fighting.

A modified version of the 415 is used for air–sea rescues and for observation roles.

The 415 has been designed to land on rough ground as well as on water.

The 415 can scoop up over 6,000 litres (1,319 gallons) of water in one go.

The plane's ability to fly at low speed helps to make sure it drops its load on the right spot.

The trouble with forest fires is that they are usually a long way from the nearest fire hydrant. This means fire crews have nowhere to plug their hoses in. This is where the 415 comes into its own. Once it has dropped its load it can simply fly to the nearest lake or sea and scoop up another load of water before dashing back to the flames.

To scoop up water, the 415 flies along the surface of the lake or sea until its two tanks are full. It is nicknamed the 'superscooper'.

SUPER STATS

BOMBARDIER 415
LENGTH: 19.8 m (65 ft)
WINGSPAN: 28.6 m (93 ft 11 ins)
RANGE: not known
NUMBER OF CREW: 2
NUMBER OF PASSENGERS: 8
TOP SPEED: 333 km/h (207 mph)

PITTS SPECIAL S-2C

Aerobatic displays are incredible spectacles in which planes perform mid-air stunts. The daredevil pilots fly in tight formations, loop the loop, and narrowly miss each other. These displays draw huge crowds – whether they feature jet planes or superplanes like Pitts Specials.

The Pitts Specials have won more aerobatic competitions in the USA than any other type of aircraft.

The Pitts Special is so stable that it can be flown in a straight line without the pilot needing to touch the hand controls.

Although they look old fashioned, the Pitts stunt planes are in fact very modern. Like the earliest planes, they have two sets of wings. The extra wings slow the planes down, but give them more lift. And the Pitts Specials use all this lift to perform amazing stunts!

It may be small, but the Pitts Special is incredibly tough. Its rigid body is ideal for twisting and turning through the sky.

The original versions of the Pitts Special had only one seat. Later versions had two, so passengers could enjoy the thrills too.

Spinning the plane around in mid-air is a popular stunt. The Pitts Special does this very quickly – it can spin 300° every second.

SUPER STATS

PITTS SPECIAL S-2C
LENGTH: 5.72 m (18 ft 9 ins)
WINGSPAN: 6.1 m (20 ft)
RANGE: 457 km (284 miles)
NUMBER OF CREW: 1
NUMBER OF PASSENGERS: 1
TOP SPEED: 313 km/h (194 mph)

ZIVKO EDGE 540

Aerobatic displays are really exciting. But what if you want even more skills and thrills? Then perhaps you should check out air racing. This mixes aerobatic ability with a race around a course! The Zivko Edge 540 has won more championships than any other type of racing plane.

Plane wings have flaps called ailerons. These help the plane to steer. The Edge has long flaps for extra manoeuvrability.

During the race, the planes have to fly through inflatable 20 m (65 ft) pylons called 'air gates'.

The planes are fitted with cameras which broadcast live during the races.

The Red Bull Air Race series ran from 2003 to 2010. The series staged races right across the globe. The races featured planes trying to navigate their way round a 5–6 km (3–4 mile) course in the fastest time possible. The Zivko Edge 540 was the most successful type of plane to compete.

The race planes leave smoke trails. These are made by injecting fuel onto the exhaust pipes.

The Edge has a very strong body to cope with the pressures of the twisting and turning during a race.

SUPER STATS

ZIVKO EDGE 540
LENGTH: 6.3 m (20 ft 8 ins)
WINGSPAN: 7.43 m (24 ft 5 ins)
RANGE: Not known
NUMBER OF CREW: 1
NUMBER OF PASSENGERS: 0
TOP SPEED: 426 km/h (265 mph)

LOCKHEED MARTIN F-22 RAPTOR

For some pilots, flying a superplane can be a matter of life and death – quite literally. Air force pilots take control of warplanes designed for aerial combat. It's a dangerous job, and not for the faint-hearted. The F-22 Raptor is a warplane flown by the United States Air Force.

The body and frame of the F-22 is made with titanium, which is a very light, but very strong metal.

The F-22 carries missiles for attacking other planes or targets on the ground.

The plane can cruise at speeds of around Mach 1.5. This means it can travel quickly without using a lot of fuel.

Two companies, Lockheed Martin and Boeing, made the F-22 together. It is a fighter plane, built to attack other aircraft or targets on the ground. It is unbelievably quick and highly manoeuvrable. Twisting and turning through the air at high speed puts a lot of strain on its tough frame.

There are fuel tanks in the wings.

Two super-powerful engines provide more thrust than its rivals.

The F-22 is designed to be difficult to spot on radar.

SUPER STATS

LOCKHEED MARTIN F-22 RAPTOR
LENGTH: 18.9 m (62 ft)
WINGSPAN: 13.56 m (44 ft 6 ins)
RANGE: (estimated) 3,000 km (1,864 miles)
NUMBER OF CREW: 1
NUMBER OF PASSENGERS: 0
TOP SPEED: 2,450 km/h (1,522 mph)

VIRGIN GALACTIC SPACESHIP TWO

SpaceShip Two does something really remarkable – it flies so high that it reaches the edge of space itself. At this distance from the Earth, gravity is not as strong. Passengers are able to float around inside!

SpaceShip Two is carried high into the sky by another plane called WhiteKnight Two. This helps to save rocket fuel.

At 15,240 m (50,000 ft) SpaceShip Two uses its rocket engines to blast off to the edge of space.

The most exciting thing about SpaceShip Two is its passengers.
Until now, the only people to have travelled so high above the Earth have been highly trained astronauts. SpaceShip Two gives ordinary people the opportunity to fly right to the edge of space!

You might have to win the lottery before you can travel on SpaceShip Two. It costs around £124,000 for a flight!

The planes take off from a special airport called Spaceport America, in New Mexico, USA.

SUPER STATS

VIRGIN GALACTIC SPACESHIP TWO
LENGTH: 18.28 m (60 ft)
WINGSPAN: 8.2 m (26 ft 10 ins)
RANGE: Not available
NUMBER OF CREW: 2
NUMBER OF PASSENGERS: 6
TOP SPEED: 3,675 km/h (2,284 mph)

SUPER

Trucks are the heavyweight champs of the highway. They are bigger and tougher than other vehicles and are used for all sorts of important jobs - and for all sorts of destructive fun!

TRUCKS

MACK TITAN
ROAD TRAIN

You need a very hardy vehicle to transport goods across vast distances. And trucks don't get any bigger or tougher than the super-long road trains.

Road trains usually pull between two and four trailers. All sorts of goods are carried, from cars to cattle, and from fuel to food.

In 2006 a Mack Titan truck pulled 113 trailers at once – a world record!

Australia is a big country, and its population is scattered over a huge area. It is expensive to transport goods across the country, because of fuel costs over long distances. The solution is road trains. These are really long trucks, which can carry far more than a normal truck.

Road trains have huge, powerful engines, but their power is used for pulling, not for speed.

The top speed of the Titan is a measly 75 km/h (46 mph).

SUPER STATS

MACK TITAN
LENGTH: 7.95 m (26 ft)
HEIGHT: 4.2 m (13 ft 9 ins)
WEIGHT: 8970 kg (197 short tons)
ENGINE: 605 bhp
TOP SPEED: 75 km/h (46 mph)

BIGFOOT MONSTER TRUCK

Monster trucks are like pick-up trucks, but with a big twist. They have huge wheels and massive tyres – more than big enough to drive right over anything that gets in their way. People come from far and wide to see them.

Bigfoot 17 is the only version of Bigfoot based in Europe full-time.

Bigfoot 17 can travel at 129 km/h (80 mph) and can jump a line of cars from a ramp.

The people who build the Bigfoot trucks must be superstitious. There has never been a Bigfoot 13.

Monster trucks perform in special shows.
They race against each other or crush cars under their massive wheels. Several famous monster trucks have been called Bigfoot. There have actually been 18 versions of Bigfoot – and they have won 29 championships between them.

Bigfoot 5 has the biggest wheels of any monster truck. The tyres alone are 3 metres (9.8 ft) tall. It's also the widest truck around.

Bigfoot 5 weighs around 12,700 kg (28,000 lbs), making it the heaviest monster truck in the world.

Bigfoot 5 is on permanent display outside a garage in St Louis, USA.

SUPER STATS

BIGFOOT 17
LENGTH: 5.5 m (18 ft)
HEIGHT: 3 m (10 ft)
WEIGHT: 4,309 kg (9,500 lbs)
WHEELS: 4
ENGINE: 1750 bhp (estimated)
TOP SPEED: 129 km/h (80 mph)

ROBOSAURUS

The biggest and best monster trucks are stars in their own right. They try to outdo each other to be the most outrageous. Some can transform into weird-looking creatures. The car-eating Robosaurus is a monster truck in every sense!

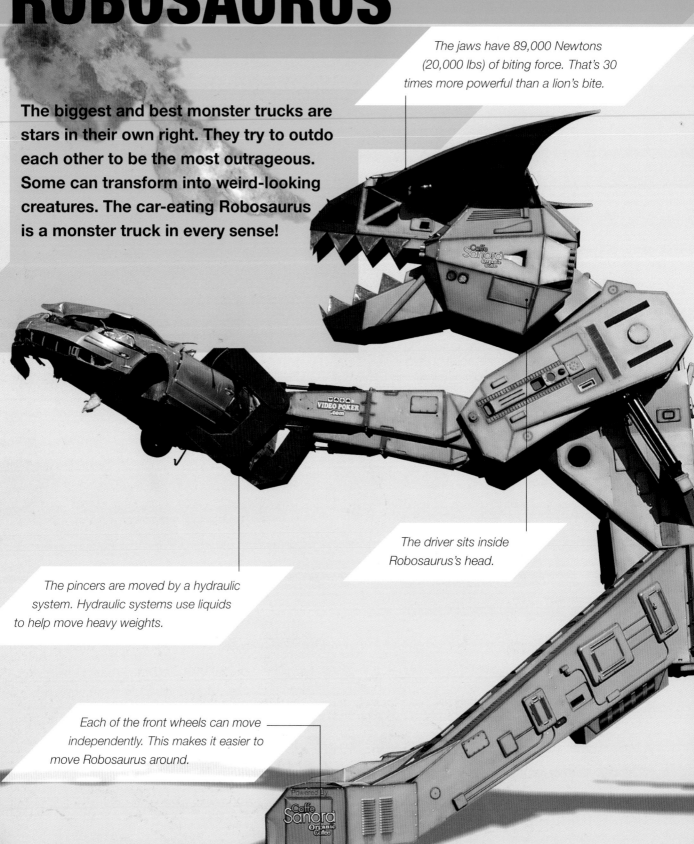

The jaws have 89,000 Newtons (20,000 lbs) of biting force. That's 30 times more powerful than a lion's bite.

The driver sits inside Robosaurus's head.

The pincers are moved by a hydraulic system. Hydraulic systems use liquids to help move heavy weights.

Each of the front wheels can move independently. This makes it easier to move Robosaurus around.

Robosaurus is a 12-metre- (40-ft-) high terror-truck. It can crush cars in its vice-like grip, or chew them to pieces in its powerful jaws. It can even breathe fire, as if it were a metal-plated dragon. Like any other truck, Robosaurus has wheels for moving about. However, it is not going to win any races!

Robosaurus can fold up like a real-life Transformer and turn into a trailer unit. It can then be attached to another truck and can be towed from place to place.

SUPER STATS

ROBOSAURUS

LENGTH: (in trailer mode)
  14.26 m (46 ft 9 inches)

HEIGHT: 12.2 m (40 ft)

WEIGHT: 26,308 kg (58,000 lbs)

WHEELS: 12

ENGINE: 500 bhp

TOP SPEED: Unknown – but very slow!

LIEBHERR T 282 C

You need a truly massive truck to take on the toughest jobs — jobs such as working in a quarry. Quarrying is a type of mining where the top layer of the ground is dug away. Giant machines are used for digging itself, and equally huge vehicles are needed to move all the rubble away.

The 282 C can carry a load of up 363 tonnes (400 tons).

The driver needs cameras and monitors to help him see what is around the truck.

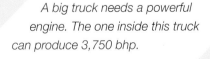

A big truck needs a powerful engine. The one inside this truck can produce 3,750 bhp.

The 282 C stands over 8 metres (26 feet) high and is over 9.5 metres (31 feet) wide.

The Liebherr T 282 C is no ordinary dump truck. This mammoth machine's job is to carry away the rocks, gravel and soil dug up by excavators. The bigger the dump truck, the more soil it can carry. As the biggest dump truck around, the T 282 C can carry 30 times more soil than normal dumpers.

The truck might be big, but it isn't fast. It has a top speed of only 65 km/h (40 mph).

Powerful hydraulics tip the back of the truck upwards to empty it.

SUPER STATS

LIEBHERR T 282 C
LENGTH: 15.69 m (51 ft 6 ins)
HEIGHT: 8.29 m (27 ft 3 ins)
WEIGHT: 237 tonnes (261 short tons)
WHEELS: 6
ENGINE: 3750 bhp
TOP SPEED: 65 km/h (40 mph)

ROSENBAUER PANTHER

The most awesome supertrucks don't just transport goods – they save lives. Giant rescue vehicles such as the Rosenbauer Panther firetruck come with all sorts of special equipment. The Panther has floodlights, hoses, huge water tanks and an extending turret!

Speed is of the essence when tackling fires. The cab is designed so that the six crew members can get out in under ten seconds.

A powerful 665 bhp engine can push the Panther to speeds of 120 km/h (75 mph) – which is fast for a big, heavy truck.

Nozzles beneath the truck can put out fires that are on the ground.

Big wheels help the Panther to travel over grass or rough terrain if necessary.

Hard-to-reach fires can be tackled by an extending turret. This can reach up to 16 metres (52 feet) high.

The Rosenbauer Panther is very different from the average firetruck. The Panther has been designed especially for airports. It is perfectly adapted for speeding down runways and for tackling the sorts of fire that might break out on an aircraft.

The Panther has large tanks for carrying foam and water.

Hoses are rewound electronically once the fire is out.

SUPER STATS

ROSENBAUER PANTHER 6X6
LENGTH: 11.83 m (38 ft 9 ins)
HEIGHT: 3.6 m (11 ft 10 ins)
WEIGHT: 31,000 kg (68,343 lbs)
WHEELS: 6
ENGINE: 665 bhp
TOP SPEED: 120 km/h (75 mph)

OSHKOSH PLS

Trucks transport goods all over the globe, using road networks. But what happens when roads have been badly damaged, or no roads exist? Well, then you need a truck that can tackle tough terrain – a truck that dares to go places others wouldn't dream of. You need the Oshkosh PLS.

The PLS is used to carry everything from ammunition to food.

Big wheels are ideal for travelling over rough ground.

The PLS (Palletised Load System) can also tow a specially designed trailer unit. This trailer can also hold loads of up to 16,000 kg (35,274 lbs) in weight.

The Oshkosh PLS is used by the armed forces. This often means that it has to deal with some really hostile environments. The terrain might be rough, so the PLS has to be good at travelling off-road. Plus the truck might be working in a war zone, so it has to be built to keep its driver as safe as possible.

The PLS has a special arm at the back. This is used for dragging containers on board. This can be done without the driver leaving the cab.

Armour-plating can be added to the cab unit.

The engine sends power to all ten wheels. This helps to keep the PLS moving when travelling off-road.

SUPER STATS

OSHKOSH PLS
LENGTH: 11 m (36 ft)
HEIGHT: 3.28 m (10 ft 9 ins)
WEIGHT: 24,834 kg (54,750 lbs)
WHEELS: 10
ENGINE: 500 bhp
TOP SPEED: 92 km/h (57 mph)

LIEBHERR LTM 11200-9.1 MOBILE CRANE

When it comes to lifting and moving heavy objects, there's no better machine than a crane. However, cranes take a long time to put up, and just as long to take down. What's the solution if you're in a hurry? A mobile crane, like the LTM 11200-9.1, could be the answer.

Cranes would topple over unless they had a weight called a 'counterweight' to balance them. This crane's counterweight weighs 201,848 kg (445,000 lbs).

The amount of weight the crane can carry depends on how far it has to reach out. The further it has to reach, the lighter the load has to be.

The boom (the crane's arm) is telescopic, which means its parts can slide into each other.

The Liebherr LTM 11200-9.1 has the longest telescopic boom in the world. It can stretch up to 100 m (328 feet) into the air! As a mobile crane, the LTM 11200-9.1 can be set up very quickly. It can also work in a much smaller space than a normal crane.

The rear wheels can be steered too, to help move the crane around tight spots.

This crane lifts loads of up to 1,200 tonnes (1,323 short tons).

SUPER STATS

LIEBHERR LTM 11200-9.1
LENGTH: 19.94 m (65 ft 5 ins)
HEIGHT: 4 m (13 ft)
WEIGHT: 96,000 kg (211,644 lbs)
WHEELS: 18
ENGINE: 680 bhp
TOP SPEED: 75 km/h (47 mph)

PISTENBULLY 600 W

The wheel may be one of the greatest inventions in history, but wheels are useless in snow. Trucks called snowcats have a clever way of dealing with this: caterpillar tracks. The PistenBully 600 W is a snowcat used for maintaining ski slopes. It can tackle deep snow and steep hills.

The tracks are made from steel or steel and rubber combined.

This winch attachment makes it easier to push large amounts of snow uphill.

Snowcats can have either two sets of tracks or four. Four-track snowcats are more manoeuvrable.

The problem with wheels and snow is surface area. The weight of a truck is carried by the parts of the tyres touching the ground. This is too much weight on too small an area for a soft surface like snow. The result is that the truck sinks.

Work on ski slopes is often done at night when the skiers have gone. Powerful lights make working in the dark much easier.

The PistenBully 600 W comes with a snowplough attachment at the front and a winch at the back.

SUPER STATS

PISTENBULLY 600 W
LENGTH: 9.13 m (30 ft)
HEIGHT: (without winch) 2.88 m (9 ft 5 ins)
WEIGHT: (with steel tracks) 11,215 kg (24,725 lbs)
WHEELS: two caterpillar tracks
ENGINE: 400 bhp
TOP SPEED: 20 km/h (12 mph)

MAN RACING TRUCK

Drivers often complain about getting stuck behind slow-moving trucks on busy roads. However, not all trucks move like snails. Some trucks are even built for racing! They compete on racing circuits in front of cheering crowds. It takes a real supertruck to do well in this battle of the titans.

MAN trucks have won the European Truck Racing Championships 11 times.

Normal road-going trucks have their engines right at the front. Race trucks move the engines further back to keep the truck balanced.

Racing rules insist that trucks have their speed limited to 161 km/h (100 mph).

Truck racing used to be between normal road-going trucks. Slowly the sport has developed and now truck manufacturers compete against each other. Racing is good publicity for truck makers – especially if their trucks are winning. One of the most successful manufacturers is the German truck maker MAN.

The trucks don't race with the trailer attached!

Special strengthening bars, called a roll cage, must be fitted to the cab in case of the truck tipping over.

Many engines have turbochargers. These push more air into the engine, which increases the engine's power.

Race trucks' engines are twice as powerful as normal road trucks' engines.

SUPER STATS

MAN RACING TRUCK
LENGTH: (estimated) 6.2 m (20 ft 4 ins)
HEIGHT: (estimated) 3 m (9 ft 8 ins)
WEIGHT: 5,500 kg (12,125 lbs)
WHEELS: 6
ENGINE: 1,000 bhp
TOP SPEED: 161 km/h (100 mph)

Jostling for position between trucks often leads to bashing and crashing, although this is officially discouraged.

SHOCKWAVE

Racing trucks may be fast, but they are not the fastest trucks around – not by a long way. For a really fast truck, you need to check out Shockwave. This jet-powered speed machine was originally a normal truck made by a company called Peterbilt. It's had a lot of changes!

The type of jet engines that power Shockwave have also been used in planes used to train jet pilots.

Shockwave won its world record by travelling at an unbelievable 605 km/h (376 mph) – that's faster than a Formula 1 grand prix car!

Shockwave travels so fast that it needs two parachutes to help slow it down.

Shockwave holds the record for being the world's fastest truck. It can achieve truly blistering speeds thanks to its super-powerful jet engines. Jet engines squash air and fuel together to generate enormous power. And just for good measure, Shockwave has three of them!

By burning diesel fuel, Shockwave can make an impressive fire display!

The engines are tilted upwards at a slight angle to help keep Shockwave from lifting off the ground.

Shockwave is a popular attraction at monster truck shows and air shows.

SUPER STATS

SHOCKWAVE

LENGTH: 6.6 m (21 ft 8 ins)
HEIGHT: Not known
WEIGHT: 3175 kg (7,000 lbs)
WHEELS: 6
ENGINE: 36,000 bhp
TOP SPEED: 605 km/h (376 mph)

HUMVEE

Tough situations call for tough trucks. Soldiers often find themselves in seriously dangerous places. They need trucks that are as at home driving off-road as they are rolling down the highway. Fortunately for the army, there's a truck that meets their needs. It's called the Humvee.

The Humvee can drive through water over 1.5 metres (4.9 ft) deep.

The engine sends power to all four wheels – this is called four-wheel drive.

Big chunky tyres provide lots of grip on slippery or loose surfaces. Slopes of up to 60% are no problem for the Humvee.

The real name for the Humvee is the HMMWV. That stands for 'High Mobility Multipurpose Wheeled Vehicle'. The Humvee's reputation for being rugged and reliable meant people who weren't in the army wanted to own one too. As a result, a civilian version was made. It is called the Hummer.

The first person to own a Hummer was actor Arnold Schwarzenegger. It was his idea to ask the Humvee manufacturers to make a civilian version.

Hummers were liked and loathed in equal measure. People loved their off-road ability, but hated their width and the amount of fuel they used.

Production of the Hummers stopped in 2010.

SUPER STATS

HMMWV M1165A1
LENGTH: 4.93 m (16 ft 2 ins)
HEIGHT: 1.91 m (6 ft 3 ins)
WEIGHT: 3,338 kg (7360 lbs)
WHEELS: 4
ENGINE: 3,400 bhp
TOP SPEED: 113 km/h (70 mph)

PATRIA PASI

Some kinds of cargo need heavy-duty protection. When armies transport soldiers, or banks transport money, they move these valuable assets in armoured vehicles. The Patria PASI is a six-wheeled, troop transporter or ambulance.

As a troop transporter, the Patria PASI can carry seven people.

The long pole at the front is actually a flagpole.

Depending on how the Patria is set up it can weigh as much as 23,000 kg (50,706 lbs).

The body plating weighs down the Patria, so it's not fast. Its top speed is only 95 km/h (59 mph).

An armoured truck is effectively a mobile fort. It is designed to resist even the most determined attackers. The army uses heavy-duty vehicles such as Patria PASI, which can do several different jobs. In civilian life, armoured trucks can sometimes be seen carrying money or valuables from shops to banks.

The truck's casing and its windows are bulletproof.

The truck can still drive even if the tyres are punctured.

The underneath of the Patria is especially strengthened to protect it against mines.

SUPER STATS

PATRIA PASI
LENGTH: 8.47 m (27 ft 9 ins)
HEIGHT: (with tower) 3.45 m (11 ft 4 ins)
WEIGHT: 23,000 kg (50,706 lbs)
WHEELS: 6
ENGINE: 270 bhp
TOP SPEED: 95 km/h (59 mph)

CUSTOMISED TRUCKS

There are many amazing trucks in the world, but very few are truly unique. If you want something that really is one of kind, you will have to do it yourself! This is called customizing. In places such as Japan and Pakistan, they have taken this trend to a whole new level.

Despite all the changes, most dekotora are still allowed to drive on the road.

Decorations include neon lights, paintings and adding lots of pipes.

Japanese customised trucks are called 'dekotora'. This means decorated trucks. They look very high-tech and futuristic. Owners meet up at dekotora shows, which draw large crowds of spectators.

In Pakistan, old trucks are often customised by street artists. They are decorated with different materials as well as paintings. Wood, metal, plastic and reflective strips can be seen.

The trucks are covered in religious paintings, humorous sayings and pictures of the 'evil eye'.

Trucks from different regions of Pakistan use different materials in their decorations.

The customised trucks of Pakistan can take up to five weeks to decorate.

SUPER STATS

These symbols and materials are typical of different regions of Pakistan.

DECORATION	REGION
Peacocks	Punjab
Carved wooden doors	Swat
Camel bone	Sindh
Plastic	Rawalpindi
Reflective tape	Karachi

FUTURE TRUCKS

Truck manufacturers are always thinking about the future. How can they make their vehicles faster, smarter and greener? They try out their ideas with concept trucks. One of the most amazing looking designs is called the Chameleon. Its body can change size depending on what it is transporting.

The designer was inspired by the way a centipede's body is made up of different segments.

Lots of glass gives the driver a good all-round view.

Future trucks will be as aerodynamic as possible. The more easily they move through the air, the less fuel they will use.

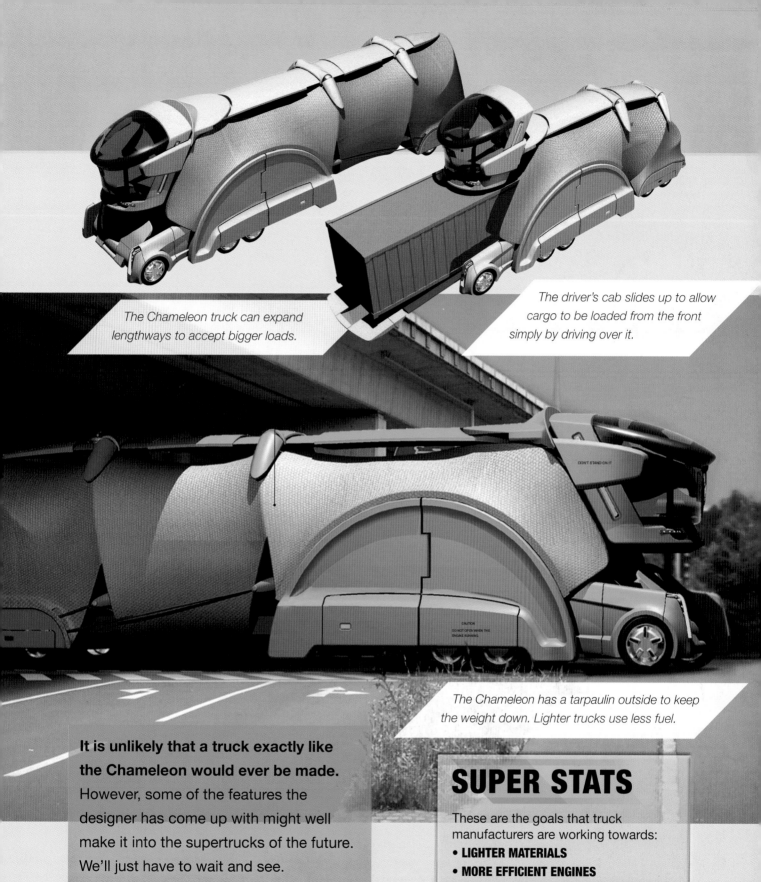

The Chameleon truck can expand lengthways to accept bigger loads.

The driver's cab slides up to allow cargo to be loaded from the front simply by driving over it.

The Chameleon has a tarpaulin outside to keep the weight down. Lighter trucks use less fuel.

It is unlikely that a truck exactly like the Chameleon would ever be made. However, some of the features the designer has come up with might well make it into the supertrucks of the future. We'll just have to wait and see.

SUPER STATS

These are the goals that truck manufacturers are working towards:
- **LIGHTER MATERIALS**
- **MORE EFFICIENT ENGINES**
- **GREENER FUELS SUCH AS HYDROGEN OR ELECTRICITY**
- **BETTER AERODYNAMIC DESIGN**

GLOSSARY

ailerons a hinged part of a plane's wing that is used to control its movement

airliner a large aircraft that carries passengers

airstrip a piece of land where planes take off and land

altitude height above the sea

aluminium a lightweight metal

bhp a measurement of the power of an engine. This stands for 'brake horsepower'.

biofuels fuels made from plants or other living things

boom a long arm, for example on a crane

booster unit a rocket that carries a craft upwards before detaching from it

carbon fibre a strong, light material made from thin rods of carbon. Carbon is also found in coal and diamonds.

caterpillar tracks wheels with a steel band around the outside, which helps them to travel across difficult terrain

chassis the base of a motor vehicle

chrome a highly reflective metal covering

concept a plan or idea

counterweight a weight that is used to stop something falling over

coupe a car with two doors and a roof

custom-made built specially for a specific customer

customise to make changes to something, so that it fits your individual needs

downforce a force that pushes a car down into the road

durable able to resist damage

excavator a digging machine

exclusive available to a small group of people, and no one else

fuselage the body of an aircraft

hostile unfriendly or dangerous

hydraulic powered by a liquid forced through tubes under pressure

hydrogen a colourless gas that is found in the air

126

level not moving up or down

Mach a measurement of speed. Mach 1 is the speed at which sound travels.

manufacturer the person or company that has made something

nitrogen a colourless gas that makes up most of the air

population the people who live in a particular area

porcelain a hard material made by heating up crushed rocks and clay

propeller a machine with spinning blades that pushes a boat or aircraft forwards

radar a high-tech system that sends out waves of energy, and uses them to detect aircraft or other vehicles and objects

range the distance that a plane can travel without landing

reinforce to make stronger

rigid able to stay the same shape, without bending

sand ladder a wide, flat piece of metal that is used to spread the weight of a car tyre and stop it getting stuck in sand

shale a soft type of rock made from layers of mud or clay

suspension the system in vehicles that stops passengers from feeling bumps

terrain the shape of an area of land, and the features of that area, such as trees

transverse positioned across something

tribute an action that shows admiration for someone or something

vice a tool with moveable jaws that can be used to hold something still

winch a machine for pulling objects up

xenon a gas used in electric lamps

PICTURE CREDITS

BW 1/13

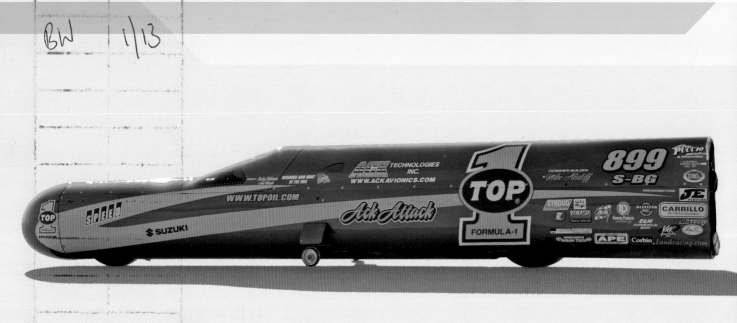